Build a Brand and Become an Expert Influencer Using Social Media Marketing

Digital
Marketing
Mastery

SOCIAL MEDIA MARKETING GUIDE

E S L A M   A L I

INTRODUCTION

Social Media Marketing is the way toward grabbing thought and web traffic through web-based life destinations. In the midst of this procedure, the commonly inventive substance to achieve the greater part through introduction starting from a pariah trusted in the source ought to be made with the true objective for individuals to impart the substance of their enthusiasm to other people and make a horrendous chain that would impact business to cover and go past the market gathering of people arranged. Each online advertiser needs a target, an item, an administration and motivation to progress through the tremendous and overwhelming World Wide Web. In the event that you start at now have those things portrayed in your psyche by then, well done! That could be no doubt the hardest bit of going into the internet based life test, and beginning now, and into the not so distant, each effort will add to achieve those goals beneficially and flawlessly until the point that you put your feet on the Social Media Guru status

The Social Media world is tremendous and more extensive than whenever in ongoing memory. It is an amazingly essential promoting stage that achieves assorted social orders, ages, religion, sexual orientations, regions, interests and such, as such it makes it the perfect vehicle to accomplish and concentrate on the right group of onlookers and gain signify ground. The whole world won't consider video

Amusements, for example, anyway simply the general population that computer games are a few their interests. On the off chance that you target male gathering of people with advancements of high foot back regions at a deal, conceivably some of them would go and buy a couple or 2 for their mates, yet a couple or 2 isn't absolutely the kind of impact you need. As such, you revolve around certain get-together ages and explicit diverse parts that reason a couple of administrations and items, recordings and news to go "viral." To begin with, we need to realize the main online life locales.

What Is Social Media Marketing?

Online life showcasing alludes to the way toward picking up traffic or consideration through internet-based life destinations.

Web-based social networking itself is a trick all term for locales that may give profoundly extraordinary social activities. For example, Twitter is a social site intended to give individuals a chance to share short messages or "updates" with others. Facebook, interestingly is an all-out informal communication site that takes into account sharing updates, photographs, joining occasions and an assortment of different exercises.

How Are Search and Social Media Marketing Related?

For what reason would an inquiry advertiser — or a site about web indexes — care about web-based life? The two are exceptionally firmly related.

Online networking frequently channels into the disclosure of new substance, for example, news stories, and "revelation" is a pursuit action. Online life can likewise help construct connects that thusly support into SEO endeavors. Numerous individuals additionally perform looks at online life destinations to discover internet-based life content. Social associations may likewise affect the importance of some list items, either inside an online networking system or at a 'standard' internet searcher.

Online life Marketing at Marketing Land

Promoting Land is the sister webpage to Search Engine Land that covers all features of web advertising, including these prominent points inside online networking showcasing:

- Facebook
- Instagram
- Twitter
- Pinterest
- LinkedIn
- YouTube
- Social Media Marketing How to Guides & more!

Welcome!

Internet-based life is a standout amongst the best correspondence and publicizing channels. Be that as it may, slicing through the clamor can be testing, and regularly, advertisers must utilize paid social showcasing systems to intensify their message in social stages.

Despite the fact that you may have made an extremely adroit bit of substance, it very well may be difficult to contact the correct group of onlookers, particularly first and foremost, where nobody knows you or your image. You can utilize social advertisements to support your current substance, for instance, your Facebook posts or your blog.

Exceptionally focused on promotions via web-based networking media can enable you to reach precisely the general population who care about your substance. The capacity to target potential per users and client's dependent on statistic information, practices, and quite certain interests is the greatest quality of web-based life promotions.

Be that as it may, social advertisements are not constrained to advancing substance; they are likewise an extraordinary method to promote items, direct people to your site or online shop, or gather contact data for your email battles.

In this guide, you realize what is conceivable in a few driving stages and figure out how to assess which stage is directly for your message and your group of onlookers. On the following pages, we spread six noteworthy web-based life stages: Facebook, Instagram, Twitter, Pinterest, Snapchat, and LinkedIn. Every one of these destinations has in excess of 100 million month to month dynamic clients.

a complete and very intelligent course that encourages all of you has to know to wind up a Digital Marketer.

Table of Contents

Table of Contents

- Facebook
- About Facebook

- What Facebook advertisements resemble

- What goals would I be able to meet with my Facebook advertisements? What focusing on choices does Facebook offer?

- What is the base spending plan to promote on Facebook? The most effective method to begin

- Contextual investigations

- Instagram

- About Instagram

- What promotion types does Instagram offer?

- What Instagram advertisements resemble

- What destinations would I be able to meet with my Instagram advertisement? What focusing on choices does Instagram offer?

- What is the base spending plan to promote on Instagram? Step by step instructions to begin

- Contextual analyses

- Twitter

- About Twitter

- What advertisement types does Twitter offer? Tweet commitment

- Video sees

- Develop your adherents

- Site visits

- Site changes

- Application introduces and re-commitment Lead age

- What focusing on choices does Twitter offer? a

- What is the base spending plan to publicize on Twitter? The most effective method to begin

- Contextual investigation

- Pinterest

- About Pinterest

- What promotion types does Pinterest offer? Mindfulness battles Engagement crusades

- Traffic crusades

- What focusing on choices does Pinterest offer?

- What is the base spending plan to promote on Pinterest? Step by step instructions to begin
- Contextual analyses

- Snapchat
- About Snapchat
- What advertisement types does Snapchat offer?
- Snapchat Discover Sponsored Lenses Snap Ads
- Supported Geofilters
- What amount do Sponsored Geofilters cost? Step by step instructions to begin

- LinkedIn
- About LinkedIn
- What advertisement types does LinkedIn offer?
- Supported Content
- Content Ads
- What focusing on choices does LinkedIn offer?

- What is the base spending plan to publicize on LinkedIn? The most effective method to begin

- Contextual analyses

- HSBC

- HP Software

Become a Digital Marketer!

Facebook

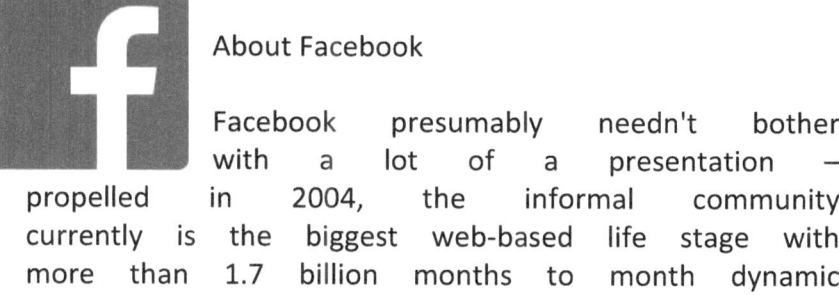

About Facebook

Facebook presumably needn't bother with a lot of a presentation – propelled in 2004, the informal community currently is the biggest web-based life stage with more than 1.7 billion months to month dynamic clients around the world. The organization today is something beyond an interpersonal organization – Facebook obtained informing application WhatsApp and began its own effective delivery person. They moreover

purchased photograph sharing stage Instagram and the augmented experience organization Oculus VR.

Since most Facebook clients sign into the site each day and draw in with different clients, brands, and substance, the stage knows a ton about their clients. For promoters, Facebook is a standout amongst the most alluring on the web channels since it gives them a chance to use their rich client information to target quite certain gatherings of people. Also, since most organizations and brands are as of now present on Facebook, promotions are an incredible method to assemble a following and lift commitment for the substance they share.

What Facebook advertisements resemble

Here you have four unique options – you can make an advertisement that includes a solitary picture, a solitary video, or various pictures that are shown either in a merry go round configuration or as a slideshow.

Single Image   Video/Slideshow   Single Carousel

Facebook likewise offers another, progressively vivid advertisement experience on a portable. They call it Facebook Canvas. Canvas resembles an ordinary versatile news source promotion, however, once a client taps to open the promotion, the individual is taken to a full-screen understanding (recordings, pictures, content, items) that the sponsor can tweak. To become familiar with Facebook Canvas, go to canvas.facebook.com.

Here is a case of how journey organization Holland America Line utilized Facebook Canvas to promote a Caribbean escape:

What targets would I be able to meet with my Facebook advertisements?

You can streamline promotions on Facebook dependent on what explicit goal your crusade has. For the most part, Facebook recognizes three various types of goals that pursue the conventional client venture from attention to change:

13

1. Raising awareness: This incorporates battles to raise brand mindfulness, neighborhood mindfulness and to augment reach.

2. Consideration: These are advertisements that direct people to your site, support the commitment of your posts, increment application downloads or video perspectives and help you gather client information (leads) to use in follow-up battles.

3. Conversion: These are promotions that expansion the change on your site or online shop*, publicize explicit items to clients who have cooperated with your shop before*, or inspire individuals to visit your neighborhood store.

*These crusade destinations expect you to include a couple of lines of code to your site, which will at that point actualize the Facebook pixel on your site. To figure out how to make a Facebook pixel and how to add it to the code of your site, see here. In the event that you need to follow the activities that occur inside your portable application because of your promotions, your engineer should actualize a bit of code called App Events. Direct them toward Facebook's developer site to find out additional.

In light of past client conduct information, Facebook will demonstrate your promotion to those individuals in your intended interest group who are well on the way to play out the activity you need them to.

What focusing on choices does Facebook offer?

Facebook offers an assortment of focusing on choices that you can consolidate to assemble a particular gathering of people:

Location	Target users by country, state, city, zip code, or the area around your physical business.
Demographics	Target users by age, gender, education, and the languages they speak.
Interests	Target users by interests, based on profile information, pages, groups or content they engage with. You can choose from hundreds of categories like sports, movies, music, games, or shopping. You can also target users who like specific pages.
Behaviors	Target users based on what Facebook knows about user behavior, such as the way they shop, the phone they use, or if they plan to buy a house or a car.
Connections	Target users who like your page or app and their friends.
Custom	Target existing customers based on data (e.g., emails, phone numbers) you provide. You can also create Lookalike Audiences - people who are similar to your existing customers.

What is the base spending plan to promote on Facebook?

When you set up your day by day spending plan on Facebook, the base everyday spending plan relies upon what your advertisement set gets charged for.

The ad set gets charged for...	Min. daily budget
Impressions	$1
Clicks, likes, video views, post engagement	$5
Offer claims, app installs and other low-frequency events	$40

In the event that you need to set up a lifetime spending plan rather, i.e., an absolute spending plan for the length of the battle, your base spending plan is determined by increasing the base everyday spending plan by the number of days the crusade endures.

Step by step instructions to begin

Click here (and after that click on "Make an Ad") to begin publicizing on Facebook, and here to get to Facebook's documentation that depicts each and every advertisement type.

Case Studies

Cupcakin' Bake Shop in Berkeley, California needed to develop its business both with customers and organizations in the region. The organization focused on its advertisement to individuals matured 18– 55, living inside 5 miles of the shop who was keen on weddings, blossoms and cupcakes. Throughout one year the crusade created 4.5X a bigger number of offers than print publicizing.

NBA group Orlando Magic needed to advance single-diversion ticket deals and chose to achieve their current database of clients and site clients utilizing Facebook's "Custom Audience" focusing on. Furthermore, they achieved neighborhood ball fans by focusing on individuals in Orlando matured 18 and more seasoned with interests in live occasions, Orlando Magic or b-ball. The crusade prompted an 84% higher profit for the cash spent ('advertisement spend') than all other publicizing channels.

Gaming organization King needed to build downloads of their versatile application diversion Candy Crush Saga. The organization tried the two promotions including a solitary picture and advertisements utilizing Facebook's merry go round arrangement with different pictures. The test demonstrated that the merry go round advertisement prompted 1.4X more Android application introduces and brought down the publicizing costs per introduce by 32%.

Instagram

About Instagram

Instagram is an on the web and versatile interpersonal organization for photograph and video-imparting to in excess of 500 million month to month dynamic clients around the world. Clients can share photographs and recordings freely and secretly on the Instagram application and through other informal communication stages, for example, Twitter, Tumblr or Facebook. Instagram began with photographs that

were square formed however at this point is available to pictures in any viewpoint proportion just as recordings with as long as 60 seconds.

For Advertisers, Instagram is an incredible stage to recount an organization's story in a visual and connecting way. Effective crusades don't move items or promote enormous limits yet bring an item's or image's real essence to life. Sponsors need to painstakingly adjust the data and the motivation estimation of their crusades to urge the network to like and share their promotions.

Since Instagram was obtained by Facebook in 2012, the publicizing stages consolidated and the greater part of the promoting and focusing on alternatives are the equivalent for the two stages. Like Facebook advertisements, to run promotions on Instagram, you'll need a Facebook Page for the brand or item you are advancing.

What ad types does Instagram offer?

Like what we have seen for Facebook, we can order Instagram's promotion alternatives dependent on what the advertisements look like and what goals they have. All Instagram promotions will be set in the client feed, both in the program and the application adaptation.

What Instagram ads look like?

Here you have a similar three options you know from Facebook

Ads – you can make an advertisement that includes a solitary photograph, a video, or **multiple photos that are displayed in a carousel format.**

Single Ad   Video Ad   Carousel Ad

What goals would I be able to meet with my Instagram promotion?

For self-administration clients, Instagram offers a scope of various goals for which you can enhance your crusade. Like Facebook, Instagram will demonstrate your promotion to the general population in your intended interest group who are well on the way to make the move you need them to take. The battle targets you can browse are:

- **Brand mindfulness**

- Reach

- Traffic (for snaps to your site or to the application store page of your application)

- App introduces

- Engagement (with your posts)

- Video sees

- Conversions (on your site or app) *

* This battle objective expects you to execute the Facebook pixel on your site. To figure out how to make a Facebook pixel and how to add it to the code of your site, see here. On the off chance that you need to follow the activities that occur inside your versatile application because of your promotions, your engineer should execute a bit of code called App Events. Guide them toward this site to find out additional.

What focusing on alternatives does Instagram offer?

Instagram offers the equivalent focusing on alternatives as Facebook. You can consolidate them to manufacture a a specific audience:

Location	Target users by country, state, city, zip code, or the area around your physical business.
Demographics	Target users by age, gender, education, and the languages they speak.
Interests	Target users by interests, based on profile information, pages or content they engage with. You can choose from hundreds of categories like sports, movies, music, games, or shopping.
Behaviors	Target users based on what Instagram knows about user behavior, such as the way they shop, the phone they use, or if they plan to buy a house or a car.
Connections	Target users who like your Facebook Page or Instagram account and their friends.
Custom	Target existing customers based on data (e.g., emails, phone numbers) you provide. You can also create Lookalike Audiences, people who are similar to your existing customers

What is the base spending plan to promote on Instagram?

The base day by day spending plan on Instagram is equivalent to for Facebook promotions and

Relies upon what your advertisement set gets charged for.

The ad set gets charged for...	Min. daily budget
Impressions	$1
Clicks, likes, video views, post engagement	$5
Offer claims, app installs and other low-frequency events	$40

On the off chance that you need to set up a lifetime spending plan rather, i.e., an absolute spending plan for the length of the battle, your base spending plan is determined by increasing the base everyday spending plan by the number of days the crusade endures.

How to get started

Instagram and Facebook utilize a similar apparatus and procedure, through Facebook's Ad Manager, to make and oversee advertisements on the two stages. Snap here (and afterward click on "Make an Ad" and pick Instagram in the Placements segment) to begin publicizing on Instagram. Snap here to get to the Instagram advertisement documentation.

Case Studies

Ben & Jerry's

Learn how ice cream brand used Instagram ads to drive sales of its new flavor, Cinnamon Bun, in Sweden by 80%.

Wool and the Gang

Fleece and the Gang is an online shop for Wool and Knitting frill that developed their business by focusing on Millennials on Instagram

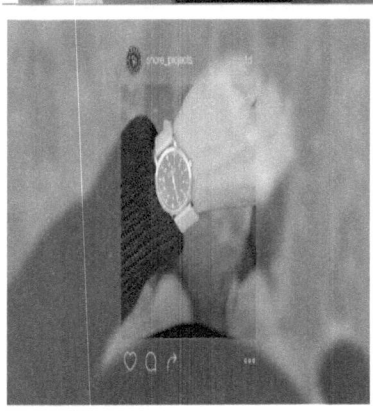

. **Shore Projects**

Watch how company Shore Projects started their business using Instagram as their only shop window. With the help of Instagram ads, they were able to turn Shore Projects into a global lifestyle brand that sells watches worldwide.

Twitter

About Twitter

Twitter, also known as the "SMS of the Internet", was founded in 2006 and now has more than 300 million registered monthly active users who post and read messages with up to 140 characters. Users can add links, photos and videos to their tweets, include hashtags to help others find their message, and run polls within a tweet.

For publicists, Twitter offers an assortment of promotion types that can be custom fitted to various battle goals, from expanding site visits and deals to making a greater after for an organization's Twitter account. Twitter likewise offers rich alternatives to focus on a particular group of onlookers, including statistic, premium and conduct focusing on.

What advertisement types does Twitter offer?

Twitter sorts out its distinctive promotion types by crusade objective: i.e., the activity a publicist needs a client to perform. Contingent upon which crusade target you pick, the advertisement will be shown in an alternate arrangement, which Twitter calls "Cards." For nitty-gritty specialized determinations of the diverse card types, investigate Twitter's documentation. Here is a diagram of the distinctive battle goals you can browse, and what the promotions look like to the client:

Tweet commitment

Advance another or existing tweet to your intended interest group. You pay for commitment with the tweet, e.g., clicks, retweets, enjoys, pursues and answers. On the off chance that you like to expand brand mindfulness and care less about commitment, you can book an Awareness

28

battle. Here you pay for the number of impressions (CPM). You can join up to four pictures to your tweet. In the event that you do this, just 116 characters are accessible for your Tweet, as 24 characters are utilized for the pictures.

Tweet without image

Tweet with one image

Tweet with multiple image

Video views

Implant a video in a tweet and elevate it to your ideal group of onlookers. Your recordings will auto-play quieted on parchment, urging clients to tap or snap to open the tweet and watch. Twitter will demonstrate your promotion as a "Video Card" that comprises of your advertisement duplicate (max. 140 characters), a video, a video title (max. 70 characters), and a video depiction (max. 200 characters). You pay for video sees, which Twitter characterizes as pursues: "A view happens when a video is in any event half in-see on the client's gadget and has been looked for something like 2 seconds, or the client snaps to watch the video in full screen."

Develop your supporters

On the off chance that you need to advance your Twitter account and develop your supporter base, this is the advertisement type for you. Twitter proposes to your intended interest group that they pursue your record, and furthermore shows whether any of their adherents pursue your record. These promotions appear in the client feed and in the

Promoted tweet with video

"Who to pursue" sidebar on Desktop. You pay for each adherent the promotion creates.

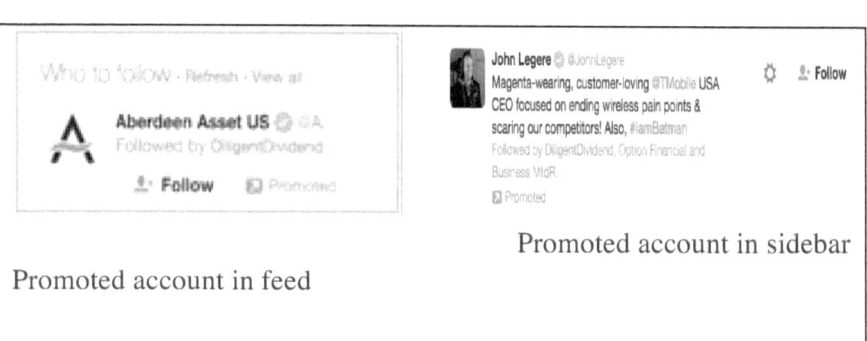

Promoted account in feed

Promoted account in sidebar

Site visits

Drive your group of onlookers to your site utilizing this crusade type. Twitter will show your message in a "Site Card" that comprises of your advertisement duplicate (max. 116 characters), a picture and a site title/portrayal (max. 70 characters). You will pay for site connect clicks.

This advertisement type makes utilization of the "Site Card" appeared, yet streamlines battles for changes, for example, buys or downloads on your site. Sponsors need to coordinate the Twitter site tag on their site, so Twitter can follow transformation. Client information about interests and goal enables Twitter to improve the battle conveyance. In spite of the fact that the goal is transformation, regardless you pay for site interface clicks.

Promoted tweet for website visits

Application introduces and re-commitment

On the off chance that your battle objective is to create downloads of your portable application or rouse individuals to open it once more, this could be an extraordinary promotion type for you. This advanced tweet is appears as an "Application Card" which comprises of a promotion duplicate (116 characters), a picture, the application name, cost and rating (pulled from the application store), and an invitation to take action catch. You can decide to either pay for application interface clicks or application introduces.

Promoted tweet for app installs

Lead generation

With the lead age battle type, you can make elevated tweets

Promoted tweet for lead generation

that plan to gather the client's email address, so you can catch up with a pamphlet or offer. The Lead Generation Card incorporates your promotion duplicate (116 characters), a Call to Action catch (20 characters), a short depiction (50 characters) and a picture. In the event that a client taps the Call to Action catch, Twitter will present the name and email related to the client's Twitter record and demonstrate an adjustable message (100 characters). You pay for the number of leads created

What targeting options does Twitter offer?

Twitter offers the following nine targeting options that you can combine as needed:

location	Target users by country, state, region, metro area, or ZIP code.
Gender	You can target only male or only female users or both. Twitter infers genders from information users share as they use Twitter, e.g., their profile names.
Languages	By default, Twitter delivers campaigns to all languages, so make sure to target only people

	who understand your message.
Devices, Platforms and Carriers	Target users who use specific mobile devices (e.g. iOS, Android, Blackberry) and mobile phone carriers (e.g. AT&T, Verizon) to access Twitter. You can also target users based on when they first used Twitter on a new device or carrier.
Interest	Target users based on 25 interest categories that expand into 350 subtopics, from Automotive to Travel. Twitter identifies user interests based on what content users engage with and what usernames they follow.
Followers	Provide Twitter with a list of usernames and your ad will reach users who have similar interests as those who follow any of the accounts you have listed.
Keyword	Reach users based on the keywords of their search queries, recent Tweets, and Tweets they recently engaged with. For each keyword, you can define whether you want to target users with exact keyword matching, broad matching (i.e., Twitter will also target related keywords) or negative matching (i.e., Twitter won't target users who match for this keyword).

Behavior	To target users based on their online and offline behavior (e.g., product or shopping preferences), Twitter utilizes user data that third-party data providers have shared with them.
Tailored Audiences	With tailored audiences, you can target existing customers, leads or website visitors. To do this, you have to upload a list of emails, Twitter IDs or mobile advertising IDs. Alternatively, you can put a code snippet on your website so Twitter can identify your website visitors. You can either focus a campaign on a tailored audience, or exclude the tailored audience if you prefer to reach only new prospects.

What is the base spending plan to publicize on Twitter?

Twitter expects you to set up a most extreme everyday spending plan for your crusades, after which Twitter will quit circulating your advertisement. Alternatively, you can likewise set the greatest spending plan for the term of the entire crusade. The expense of an activity (characterized by battle type, as clarified prior) relies upon how much different promoters, who contend with you for a similar gathering of people, offer. Dissimilar to Facebook and Instagram, Twitter does not request that you submit a base spending plan.

Step by step instructions to begin

To begin you need a functioning Twitter account. Go to Twitter Ads and you will be provoked with a screen where you select your battle objective. These destinations coordinate the ones we have examined previously. In the event that you stall out, view Twitter's documentation for Businesses.

Contextual investigation

L'Oréal Paris Australia needed to drive traffic and commitment from elite TV content around celebrity main street occasions, utilizing Twitter. To do this, the brand utilized Promoted Tweets, a Promoted Trend and a Twitter Amplify battle that guided clients to L'Oréal's Get the Look Website.

Pinterest

About Pinterest

Photograph and video sharing site Pinterest gives clients a chance to transfer, spare, sort, and compose pictures and recordings, called pins, in close to home and community-oriented accumulations, called sheets. The stage presently reports 150 million months to month dynamic clients, who add to what the Pinterest CEO calls the "List of Ideas".

Numerous organizations, particularly in the style, workmanship or inside structure space, have

38

effectively utilized Pinterest to advance their items naturally and have built up a following which draws in with their substance. Advanced Pins are Pinterest's local publicizing position – they look and carry on indistinguishable route from ordinary Pins, yet sponsors can pay to have them seen by more clients.

What advertisement types does Pinterest offer?

As of now, Pinterest just offers one publicizing type to all organizations in the US, Canada, and the UK: The Promoted Pin. The organization is additionally trying a Pin in which you can specifically purchase the item you see (Buyable Pin), however, this component is at present just accessible to a restricted group of onlookers.

Advanced Pins are embedded in a client's feed and query items. They look precisely like ordinary Pins, yet are set apart as "Advanced Pins".

You can purchase Promoted Pins streamlined for three distinctive battle destinations: Awareness, Engagement, and Traffic.

Mindfulness battles

Mindfulness battles are the correct decision if your primary goal is to get your image or item presented to whatever number individuals in your intended interest group as would be prudent. Many individuals use Pinterest to find new thoughts and get motivation without a solid arrangement as a primary concern. Mindfulness crusades get enhanced for reach, not for the commitment, and you will pay dependent on the quantity of impressions your Pins produce.

Commitment battles

In the event that you pick a commitment battle, Pinterest will streamline the conveyance of your Pins so they contact individuals who could be keen on sparing or repining them. These crusades target
 individuals who are in the 'aim' stage and who are effectively searching for answers for their issues or thoughts for their activities. This is likewise the correct crusade type if your goal is to construct a greater after on Pinterest. You will be charged for commitment (close-ups, repines or clicks), not for impressions. Note that this crusade type won't immediate clients to your point of arrival. To do this, pick traffic crusades.

Traffic battles

Traffic battles are intended to drive Pinterest clients to a publicist's point of arrival. In this way, if your goal is to target individuals who have finished the motivation and arranging stage and are prepared to act (or purchase), pick this battle type. This is the main battle type that will incorporate a connection to your point of arrival in the Promoted Pin. You will be charged for each connection click.

What focusing on alternatives does Pinterest offer?

40

Pinterest offers an assortment of focusing on choices that you can consolidate to fabricate a particular group of onlookers:

Location	Target any combination of users from the US, Canada, and the UK, at the country level or at the metro level.
Languages	Target users who speak specific languages.
Gender	Target users based on their gender.
Devices	Target users based on the specific device they use to access Pinterest.
Keywords	Target users who search for a specific keyword (which must be relevant for your ad).
Interests	Target users based on other Pins they have saved and engaged with.
Audience	Target: people who have visited your website (you have to embed a Pinterest tag in the code of your site); existing customers or leads (you have to upload a list of email addresses); an audience that has engaged with Pins that link to your website; or an 'act-alike audience' that behaves similarly to your existing audience (you need to provide a list with at least 100 email addresses of customers who are also

	Pinterest users).

What is the base spending plan to promote on Pinterest?

When you have set up a battle and entered your offer for a particular group of onlookers you target, Pinterest will give you some direction on whether your offer appears to be encouraging or not. Just mindfulness crusades require a base spending plan; the other two battle types don't require a base offer. Examine the table beneath to see how you might be charged:

Advertising objective	What your maximum bid means
Awareness	Your bid is the maximum you are willing to pay for every 1,000 people (CPM) who see your Promoted Pin. The minimum you can bid is $5.

Engagement	Your bid is the maximum you are willing to pay when a user engages with a Promoted Pin, i.e. close-ups, repines and click-through (Cost Per Engagement, CPE). Important: if a user close-ups, repines and clicks through on your Pin, you will be charged for each of these actions.
Traffic	Your bid is the maximum you are willing to pay for each click a person makes on your Promoted Pin to visit your website (CPC).

The most effective method to begin

To begin, you need a Pinterest business account (you can enlist here). You can likewise change over your current record into a business account. After you have enlisted your business account, click here to begin. In the event that you have any inquiries or issues once you begin, examine Pinterest's Help Center.

Case Studies

 [Adore Me](#) is a membership administration for present-day undergarments, focusing on millennial ladies. In the wake of building an incredible premise of adherents naturally, the organization utilized Promoted Pins to contact a greater crowd and pitch memberships to new clients. The best Pins were the point at which the model's face was not obvious, so the client could envision herself wearing the items. Venerate Me saw a 2,600% expansion in site traffic from Pinterest and higher transformations than on different channels.

REESE'S utilized Promoted Pins to drive item thought for their notable Peanut Butter Cups. The brand intended to achieve youthful clients who were arranging menus or back end occasions amid the football season. To do that, REESE'S advanced Pins highlighting one of a kind Football themed formulas to their intended interest group. A statistical surveying study demonstrated that the crusade without a doubt drove item thought and brand idealness for REESE's items.

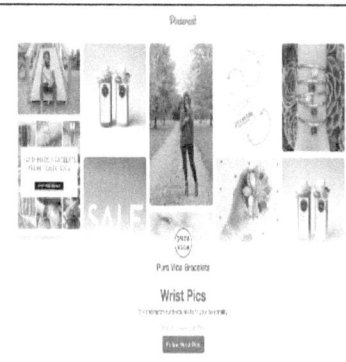

Pura Vida moves wrist trinkets made in Costa Rica in excess of 3,500 stores around the world. Before utilizing Promoted Pins, the organization utilized Pinterest to recount their organization story, share their blog entries and grandstand their items. To drive new clients to their site and expand its Pinterest fan base, the organization set up traffic and commitment battles, including their items and the way of life-related to them. 25 days after the crusade finished, Pura Vida saw an expansion in requests by 31%.

45

Snapchat

About Snapchat

Snapchat began as visual texting administration and has now advanced into a mix of a media informing and substance stage. Snapchat now has in excess of 200 million month to month dynamic clients, a significant number of them Millennials. They trade snaps and stories with their companions and access the media content given by the article

Since 2015 promoters can achieve Snapchat's clients through various advertisement arrangements and sponsorships. Most of publicizing contributions are presently just accessible to greater sponsors with extensive spending plans. Be that as it may, one promotion type, the On-Demand Geofilter, is bookable through self-administration.

What advertisement types does Snapchat offer?

A large portion of Snapchat's publicizing alternatives are focused everywhere brands and organizations, and can't be reserved through a self-administration stage like alternate choices we have seen up until now. Just Sponsored Geofilters are accessible through self-administration, so remember that while assessing publicizing channels.

Snapchat Discover

It's not formally recorded on the site; however, brands can assume control over a distributer's direct in the Discover area of the application for about $50,000 every day. In the event that you need to support a Live Story (likewise a component in the Discovery segment), you can hope to pay about $250,000.

Supported Lenses

Supported Lenses are an exceptionally intuitive organization in which clients draw in with limited time components that overlay a video client's film of her/himself. Snapchat reports that the normal client plays for 20 seconds with a Sponsored Lens, which can truly enable a brand to drive mindfulness. Taco Bell's Sponsored Lens got more than 224 million perspectives. In any case, high commitment accompanies a high sticker price: Sponsored Lenses can cost $500,000 or more – every day.

Taco Bell's Sponsored Lens on Snapchat

Snap Ads

47

Snap Ads are 10-second vertical versatile video advertisements with the choice to swipe up for progressively related substance, for example, another video, article, promotion or portable site. Snapchat says that multiple times a bigger number of clients swipe up on Snap Ads than navigate on advertisements on similar stages. Evaluating for Snap Ads relies upon the subtleties of the battle, however, can be as low as $1,000. Presently Snap Ads must be reserved through Snapchat's Partners.

Here is a precedent from Netflix, publicizing their creation LOVE:

Supported Geofilters

This is simply the main publicizing alternative you can book yourself on the web and with a little spending plan. Geofilters, in any case, is a quite certain promotion type that just suits some crusade destinations. Geofilters are pre-planned overlays,

49

for example, outlines, logos, pictures or content components that Snapchat clients can use to improve their snaps in the event that they are in a specific area. Organizations and brands can buy Geofilters for a particular area (somewhere in the range of 20,000 and 5,000,000 square feet) to advance their item, administrations or occasion.

Geofilter for Sports Event   *Geofilter for Birthday*

Likewise, huge brands like Starbucks or McDonald's make utilization of Sponsored Geofilters focusing on the areas of their stores. Thusly clients are urged to share their involvement energetically.

Starbucks Geofilter (Source)   **McDonald's Geofilter (Source)**

On the off chance that your goal is to advance a store in a shopping center, a gathering on grounds, a corner at a meeting, or whatever else that is important to Snapchat clients in a particular area, Geofilters could be a fascinating decision for you. You can likewise utilize Geofilters to make some excitement for your companions or visitors at a wedding, birthday or some other individual event. Be that as it may, on the off chance that you need to target clients in an entire city or nation, or by explicit interests or practices, this is most likely not the correct decision for you.

What amount do Sponsored Geofilters cost?

The cost of a Geofilter relies upon the dates, times and the zone estimate (estimated in square feet) of your Geofilter. Estimating starts at $5 for a Geofilter covering a little territory amid a brief timeframe, yet Snapchat will demonstrate to you a careful statement once you have entered this data in their booking stage.

The most effective method to begin

Goto https://www.snapchat.com/geofilters and sign in with your Snapchat account data. The Geofilter creation device strolls you through the structure procedure, helping you with adaptable formats. On the other hand, structure your own Geofilter in your most loved picture altering programming (e.g., Adobe Photoshop) and transfer your record (adapt more here). Pick the dates (min. 60 minutes, worst case scenario. 30 days) and characterize the area of your Geofilter (right now just

52

the US, UK, and Canada): Enter the location nearest to the region you need to publicize and draw a fence around your chose territory. Your territory must be somewhere in the range of 20,000 and 5,000,000 square feet. Snapchat then statements you a cost and you can present your request for endorsement. On the off chance that you have any inquiries, view the related segment on the Snapchat Support site.

LinkedIn

About LinkedIn

LinkedIn is the biggest expert informal organization on the planet with an excess of 460 million enlisted records. Of these, around 106 million clients visit the site at any rate once per month. Notwithstanding enabling clients to associate with one another and scan for business contacts, LinkedIn offers amass highlights, organization pages, and employment postings. They likewise have a distributing stage on which welcomed idea pioneers, influencers, and all other registered clients can distribute posts.

From a publicizing stance, LinkedIn can be an incredible stage for two purposes: To advance bosses, their occupations and stories, and to promote items and administrations that are important to an expert group of onlookers.

What promotion types does LinkedIn offer?

LinkedIn offers two sorts of advertisements – Sponsored Content and Text Ads. These advertisement types can be reserved by means of LinkedIn's self-administration stage, called Campaign Manager. Moreover, bigger publicists

54

can book show advertisements and limited time messages, called Sponsored in Mail, by means of the LinkedIn Ad Sales group. In the event that you need to become familiar with these alternatives, investigate here.

Supported Content

LinkedIn's Sponsored Content Ad enables you to distribute a special refresh on clients' newsfeeds, close by every one of the updates from their standard associations. The refresh is set apart as 'Supported,' however other than that it looks and carries on precisely like a typical refresh. Your refresh can incorporate a picture, video, infographic, PDF, Slide Share or connection to a blog entry or greeting page.

To set up a Sponsored Content Ad, you need access to a Company Page or a Showcase Page or make another one. Your substance will be partaking for the sake of this organization or brand. With a tick on the client name or symbol, individuals can visit the separate page and pursue your updates. Your Sponsored Content Ad can either advance a current refresh from your page or a refresh you make explicitly for your battle. LinkedIn gives you different focusing on alternatives to contact your ideal gathering of people, which we will cover later.

Content Ads

LinkedIn Text Ads are conventional promotions that show up in the correct segment

Ads You May Be Interested In

A 99% Employment Rate
Get recruited by all of the Big 4 and middle-market accounting firms.

Want to be a boss?
Supercharge your leadership skills with an MBA from top CEO Jack Welch.

Simple Story Videos
We add strategy to your story to create an impactful video. 1-877-513-2422.

of the work area and in different areas on their site. A Text Ad comprises of a little picture (50x50 pixels), a short feature (25 characters), a depiction (75 characters) and a connection to your point of arrival or LinkedIn Company Page.

What focusing on alternatives does LinkedIn offer?

LinkedIn gives you a chance to target clients' dependent on their socioeconomics, instruction, proficient experience, and gathering enrollments:

Demographics	Target users by age, gender and location.
Education	Target users by schools, degrees and field of study.
Experience	Target users by job function and title, seniority, skills, company name, company industry and company size.
Groups	Target users by the groups they belong to on LinkedIn.

What is the base spending plan to promote on LinkedIn?

You can set up your Sponsored Content and Text Ad battles both as a tick (CPC) or impression (CPM) based crusades. The base everyday spending plan for both advertisement types is $10.

With both crusade types, the LinkedIn Campaign Manager will demonstrate to you a recommended offer range dependent on what different publicists are offering for a similar group of onlookers. The base CPC or CPM offer for Text Ads is $2. For Sponsored Content, the base offer relies upon your intended interest group.

The most effective method to begin

To begin, get to LinkedIn's Campaign Manager by clicking here and after that click on "Make Ad'. This will give you a screen where you can choose your advertisement type. LinkedIn will at that point walk you through the advertisement creation, focusing on and planning process. In the event that you go over any issues or questions, investigate LinkedIn's Advertising FAQ's. They have likewise made a nitty-gritty Text Ad playbook, which merits looking at in the event that you intend to run Text Ads.

Contextual analyses

HSBC

Money related specialist co-op HSBC utilized LinkedIn's Sponsored Content to draw in new business clients and create more adherents with connecting with substance about working together all inclusive.

HP Software

With the assistance of LinkedIn Sponsored Content and In Mail, HP Software (Hewlett Packard) could drive a discussion among focused IT chiefs, experts and designers. The organization advanced applicable substance, provocative insights and infographics to draw in their gathering of people.

Become a Digital Marketer!

Utilize your investigative and strategic abilities to help develop and grow new open doors for organizations as a computerized advertiser. From showcasing plans and substance technique to lead age and SEO, this way manages you through the prescribed procedures and standards of computerized advertising.

Dear Reader,

First of all, thank you for purchasing this book [Social media marketing Guide]
Thank you for choosing to read my books out of the thousands that merit reading... I recognize that reading takes time and quietness, so I am grateful that you have designed your lives to allow for this enriching endeavor,
If you loved the book and have a minute to spare, I would really appreciate a short review on the page or site where you bought the book. Your help in spreading the word is greatly appreciated. Reviews from readers like you make a huge difference in helping new readers find subjects similar to [Social media marketing Guide].

. I know you could have picked any number of books to read, but you picked this book and for that, I am extremely grateful.

I hope that it added value and quality to your everyday life. If so, it would be really nice if you could share this book with your friends and family by posting to Facebook and Twitter.

If you enjoyed this book and found some benefit in reading this, I'd like to hear from you and hope that you could take some time to post a review on Amazon. Your feedback and support will help this author to greatly improve his writing craft for future projects and make this book even better.

I want you, the reader, to know that your review is very important and so if you'd like to leave a review, all you have to do is click here and away you go. I wish you all the best in your future success!
Thank you for your time!

Thank you!
[Eslam Ali]

www.ingramcontent.com/pod-product-compliance
Lightning Source LLC
Chambersburg PA
CBHW020622220526
45463CB00006B/2649